Robert Burns

Selected Poems

PENGUIN BOOKS

PENGUIN BOOKS

Published by the Penguin Group

Penguin Books Ltd, 80 Strand, London WC2R ORL, England
Penguin Group (USA) Inc., 375 Hudson Street, New York, New York 10014, USA
Penguin Group (Canada), 90 Eglinton Avenue East, Suite 700, Toronto, Ontario,
Canada M4P 2Y3 (a division of Pearson Penguin Canada Inc.)
Penguin Ireland, 25 St Stephen's Green, Dublin 2, Ireland
(a division of Penguin Books Ltd)
Penguin Group (Australia), 250 Camberwell Road, Camberwell, Victoria 3124,
Australia (a division of Pearson Australia Group Pty Ltd)
Penguin Books India Pvt Ltd, 11 Community Centre,
Panchsheel Park, New Delhi – 110 017, India
Penguin Group (NZ), cnr Airborne and Rosedale Roads, Albany,
Auckland 1310, New Zealand (a division of Pearson New Zealand Ltd)
Penguin Books (South Africa) (Pty) Ltd, 24 Sturdee Avenue,
Rosebank, Johannesburg 2196, South Africa

Penguin Books Ltd, Registered Offices: 80 Strand, London WC2R ORL, England

www.penguin.com

First published 1993
Reprinted in this edition 2006

1

The moral right of the editor has been asserted

'Ode to Spring' from James Kingsley,
ed., *The Poems and Songs of
Robert Burns*, 3 vols, 1968, are
reproduced by permission of Oxford University Press.

Typeset by Palimpsest Book Production Limited,
Polmont, Stirlingshire
Printed in England by Clays Ltd, St Ives plc

ISBN-13: 978-0-140-42468-3
ISBN-10: 0-140-42468-7

ROBERT BURNS: SELECTED POEMS

PENGUIN SELECTED

ROBERT BURNS was born in 1759, the son of a struggling tenant farmer in Ayrshire, who nevertheless joined with neighbours to employ a university-trained tutor for their children. When very young, Burns read the Bible, the English Augustans and Gray; later he immersed himself in the poetry of Milton and the sentimental fiction of Sterne. The surrounding countryside was rich in folk-lore, but the vernacular poetry of Robert Fergusson came his way only by chance and it was not until his early twenties that he real-ized the possibilities of contemporary literature in Scots. Meanwhile the privation and overwork of subsistence farming began the rheumatic heart-disease that was to cause his premature death. His father died less than a month after averting bankruptcy proceedings in 1784 and Burns, as head of the family, leased a farm at Mossgeil. He began to circulate verse satires on Calvinist extrem-ists, and in July 1786 the Church avenged itself by exacting public penance from him and Jean Armour who was pregnant by him and whom he acknowledged as his wife in 1788. *Poems, Chiefly in the Scottish Dialect* was published in 1786 and enthusiastically received and Burns spent the winters of 1786–7 and 1787–8 in Edinburgh, acting out with increasing unease the role of child of nature and untutored poet of the plough in which the Edinburgh gentry had cast him, seeking relief in the city's hard-drinking low life. An admirer leased him a farm at Ellisland and in 1789 he was appointed to the Excise Division in nearby Dumfries. The farm failed, through lack of capital and, continuing with the Excise, Burns devoted his main energies to collecting and rewriting Scots songs. He moved to Dumfries in 1791, where, despite official investiga-tion into his sympathies for the French Revolution, he was promoted in the Excise and helped to organize local Volunteer units. His health gave way and he died in 1796.

821 Bro

Contents

It Was Upon a Lammas Night

(TUNE: CORN RIGS ARE BONIE)

It was upon a Lammas night,
    When corn rigs are bonie,
Beneath the moon's unclouded light,
    I held awa to Annie:
The time flew by, wi' tentless heed,
    Till 'tween the late and early;
Wi' sma' persuasion she agreed,
    To see me thro' the barley.

The sky was blue, the wind was still,
    The moon was shining clearly;
I set her down, wi' right good will,
    Amang the rigs o' barley:
I ken't her heart was a' my ain;
    I lov'd her most sincerely;
I kiss'd her owre and owre again,
    Amang the rigs o' barley.

I lock'd her in my fond embrace;
    Her heart was beating rarely:
My blessings on that happy place,
    Amang the rigs o' barley!
But by the moon and stars so bright,
    That shone that hour so clearly!
She ay shall bless that happy night,
    Amang the rigs o' barley.

I hae been blythe wi' comrades dear;
    I hae been merry drinking;
I hae been joyfu' gath'rin gear;
    I hae been happy thinking;
But a' the pleasures e'er I saw,
    Tho' three times doubl'd fairly,

That happy night was worth them a',
   Amang the rigs o' barley.

Corn rigs, an' barley rigs,
   An' corn rigs are bonie:
I'll ne'er forget that happy night
   Amang the rigs wi' Annie.

Song Composed in August

(TUNES: I HAD A HORSE, I HAD NAE MAIR;
PORT GORDON)

Now westlin winds, and slaught'ring guns
   Bring Autumn's pleasant weather;
And the moorcock springs, on whirring wings,
   Amang the blooming heather:
Now waving grain, wide o'er the plain,
   Delights the weary farmer;
And the moon shines bright, when I rove at night,
   To muse upon my charmer.

The partridge loves the fruitful fells;
   The plover loves the mountains;
The woodcock haunts the lonely dells;
   The soaring hern the fountains:
Thro' lofty groves, the cushat roves,
   The path of man to shun it;
The hazel bush o'erhangs the thrush,
   The spreading thorn the linnet.

Thus ev'ry kind their pleasure find,
   The savage and the tender;
Some social join, and leagues combine;
   Some solitary wander;
Avaunt, away! the cruel sway,
   Tyrannic man's dominion;
The sportsman's joy, the murd'ring cry,
   The flutt'ring, gory pinion!

But Peggy dear, the ev'ning's clear,
   Thick flies the skimming swallow;
The sky is blue, the fields in view,
   All fading-green and yellow:
Come let us stray our gladsome way,

And view the charms of nature;
The rustling corn, the fruited thorn,
    And ev'ry happy creature.

We'll gently walk, and sweetly talk,
    Till the silent moon shine clearly;
I'll grasp thy waist, and fondly prest,
    Swear how I love thee dearly:
Not vernal show'rs to budding flow'rs,
    Not autumn to the farmer,
So dear can be, as thou to me,
    My fair, my lovely charmer!

John Barleycorn*
A Ballad

(TUNES: COLD AND RAW; LULL ME BEYOND THEE)

There was three kings into the east,
    Three kings both great and high,
And they hae sworn a solemn oath
    John Barleycorn should die.

They took a plough and plough'd him down,
    Put clods upon his head,
And they hae sworn a solemn oath
    John Barleycorn was dead.

But the chearful spring came kindly on,
    And show'rs began to fall;
John Barleycorn got up again,
    And sore surpris'd them all.

The sultry suns of summer came,
    And he grew thick and strong,
His head weel arm'd wi' pointed spears,
    That no one should him wrong.

The sober autumn enter'd mild,
    When he grew wan and pale;
His bending joints and drooping head
    Show'd he began to fail.

His colour sicken'd more and more,
    He faded into age;
And then his enemies began
    To show their deadly rage.

They've taen a weapon, long and sharp,
    And cut him by the knee;

* This is partly composed on the plan of an old song known by the same name. [RB]

Then ty'd him fast upon a cart,
  Like a rogue for forgerie.

They laid him down upon his back,
  And cudgell'd him full sore;
They hung him up before the storm,
  And turn'd him o'er and o'er.

They filled up a darksome pit
  With water to the brim,
They heaved in John Barleycorn,
  There let him sink or swim.

They laid him out upon the floor,
  To work him farther woe,
And still, as signs of life appear'd,
  They toss'd him to and fro.

They wasted, o'er a scorching flame,
  The marrow of his bones;
But a miller us'd him worst of all,
  For he crush'd him between two stones.

And they hae taen his very heart's blood,
  And drank it round and round;
And still the more and more they drank,
  Their joy did more abound.

John Barleycorn was a hero bold,
  Of noble enterprise,
For if you do but taste his blood,
  'Twill make your courage rise.

'Twill make a man forget his woe;
  'Twill heighten all his joy:
'Twill make the widow's heart to sing,
  Tho' the tear were in her eye.

Then let us toast John Barleycorn,
  Each man a glass in hand;
And may his great posterity
  Ne'er fail in old Scotland!

Green Grow the Rashes. A Fragment

(TUNE: GREEN GROWS THE RASHES)

CHORUS

Green grow the rashes, O;
Green grow the rashes, O;
The sweetest hours that e'er I spend,
 Are spent amang the lasses, O.

There's nought but care on ev'ry han',
 In ev'ry hour that passes, O:
What signifies the life o' man,
 An' 'twere na for the lasses, O?
  Green grow, &c.

The warly race may riches chase,
 An' riches still may fly them, O;
An' tho' at last they catch them fast,
 Their hearts can ne'er enjoy them, O.
  Green grow, &c.

But gie me a canny hour at e'en,
 My arms about my Dearie, O;
An' warly cares, an' warly men,
 May a' gae tapsalteerie, O!
  Green grow, &c.

For you sae douse, ye sneer at this,
 Ye're nought but senseless asses, O:
The wisest Man the warl' saw,
 He dearly lov'd the lasses, O.
  Green grow, &c.

Auld Nature swears, the lovely Dears
 Her noblest work she classes, O:
Her prentice han' she try'd on man,
 An' then she made the lasses, O.
  Green grow, &c.

A Poet's Welcome to His Love-Begotten Daughter;
The First Instance that Entitled Him to the
Venerable Appellation of Father

Thou's welcome wean, mischanter fa' me,
If thoughts o' thee, or yet thy Mamie,
Shall ever daunton me, or awe me,
   My sweet wee lady,
Or if I blush when thou shalt ca' me
   Tit-ta or daddy.

What tho' they ca' me fornicator,
An' tease my name in kintry clatter:
The mair they tauk I'm kent the better,
   E'en let them clash;
An auld wife's tongue's a feckless matter
   To gie ane fash.

Welcome, my bonie, sweet, wee dochter!
Tho' ye come here a wee unsought for,
And tho' your comin I hae fought for
   Baith kirk and queir;
Yet, by my faith, ye're no unwrought for –
   That I shall swear!

Wee image of my bonny Betty,
I fatherly will kiss and daut thee,
As dear an' near my heart I set thee
   Wi' as gude will
As a' the priests had seen me get thee
   That's out o' hell.

Sweet fruit o' mony a merry dint,
My funny toil is no a' tint;
Tho' ye came to the warl asklent,
   Which fools may scoff at;
In my last plack thy part's be in't,
   The better ha'f o't.

Tho' I should be the waur bestead,
Thou's be as braw and bienly clad,
And thy young years as nicely bred
        Wi' education,
As onie brat o' wedlock's bed
          In a' thy station.

Gude grant that thou may ay inherit
Thy mither's looks, and gracefu' merit;
An' thy poor worthless dady's spirit,
        Without his failins,
'Twill please me mair to see thee heir it
          Than stocket mailens.

An' if thou be what I wad ha'e thee,
An' tak the counsel I sall gi'e thee,
A lovin' father I'll be to thee,
        If thou be spar'd;
Thro' a' thy childish years I'll e'e thee,
          An' think't weel war'd.

To a Mouse
On Turning Her up in Her Nest with the Plough,
November 1785

Wee, sleeket, cowran, tim'rous *beastie*,
O, what a panic's in thy breastie!
Thou need na start awa sae hasty,
          Wi' bickering brattle!
I wad be laith to rin an' chase thee,
          Wi' murd'ring *pattle*!

I'm truly sorry Man's dominion
Has broken Nature's social union,
An' justifies that ill opinion,
          Which makes thee startle,
At me, thy poor, earth-born companion,
          An' *fellow-mortal*!

I doubt na, whyles, but thou may thieve;
What then? poor beastie, thou maun live!
A *daimen-icker* in a *thrave*
          'S a sma' request:
I'll get a blessin wi' the lave,
          An' never miss't!

Thy wee-bit *housie*, too, in ruin!
It's silly wa's the win's are strewin!
An' naething, now, to big a new ane,
          O' foggage green!
An' bleak December's winds ensuin,
          Baith snell an' keen!

Thou saw the fields laid bare an' wast,
An' weary Winter comin fast,
An' cozie here, beneath the blast,
          Thou thought to dwell,

Till crash! the cruel *coulter* past
                Out thro' thy cell.

That wee-bit heap o' leaves an' stibble,
Has cost thee monie a weary nibble!
Now thou's turn'd out, for a' thy trouble,
                But house or hald,
To thole the Winter's sleety dribble,
                An' *cranreuch* cauld!

But Mousie, thou art no thy-lane,
In proving *foresight* may be vain:
The best laid schemes o' *Mice* an' *Men*,
                Gang aft agley,
An' lea'e us nought but grief an' pain,
                For promis'd joy!

Still, thou art blest, compar'd wi' *me*!
The *present* only toucheth thee:
But Och! I *backward* cast my e'e,
                On prospects drear!
An' *forward*, tho' I canna *see*,
                I *guess* an' *fear*!

To a Louse
On Seeing One on a Lady's Bonnet at Church

Ha! whare ye gaun, ye crowlan ferlie!
Your impudence protects you sairly:
I canna say but ye strunt rarely,
        Owre *gawze* and *lace*;
Tho' faith, I fear ye dine but sparely,
        On sic a place.

Ye ugly, creepan, blastet wonner,
Detested, shunn'd, by saunt an' sinner,
How daur ye set your fit upon her,
        Sae fine a *Lady*!
Gae somewhere else and seek your dinner,
        On some poor body.

Swith, in some beggar's haffet squattle;
There ye may creep, and sprawl, and sprattle,
Wi' ither kindred, jumping cattle,
        In shoals and nations;
Whare *horn* nor *bane* ne'er daur unsettle,
        Your thick plantations.

Now haud you there, ye're out o' sight,
Below the fatt'rels, snug and tight,
Na faith ye yet! ye'll no be right,
        Till ye've got on it,
The vera tapmost, towrin height
        O' *Miss's bonnet*.

My sooth! right bauld ye set your nose out,
As plump an' gray as onie grozet:
O for some rank, mercurial rozet,
        Or fell, red smeddum,
I'd gie you sic a hearty dose o't,
        Wad dress your droddum!

I wad na been surpriz'd to spy
You on an auld wife's *flainen toy*;
Or aiblins some bit duddie boy,
   On's *wylecoat*;
But Miss's fine *Lunardi*, fye!
   How daur ye do't?

O Jenny dinna toss your head,
An' set your beauties a' abroad!
Ye little ken what cursed speed
   The blastie's makin,
Thae *winks* and *finger-ends*, I dread,
   Are notice takin!

O wad some Pow'r the giftie gie us
To see oursels as others see us!
It wad frae monie a blunder free us
   An' foolish notion:
What airs in dress an' gait wad lea'e us,
   And ev'n Devotion!

Address to the Deil

O Prince, O chief of many throned pow'rs,
That led th' embattl'd Seraphim to war —
                                    Milton

O Thou, whatever title suit thee!
Auld Hornie, Satan, Nick, or Clootie!
Wha in yon cavern grim an' sootie,
                    Clos'd under hatches,
Spairges about the brunstane cootie,
                    To scaud poor wretches!

Hear me, *auld Hangie*, for a wee,
An' let poor, *damned bodies* bee;
I'm sure sma' pleasure it can gie,
                    Ev'n to a *deil*,
To skelp an' scaud poor dogs like me,
                    An' hear us squeel!

Great is thy pow'r, an' great thy fame;
Far kend an' noted is thy name;
An' tho' yon *lowan heugh's* thy hame,
                    Thou travels far;
An' faith! thou's neither lag nor lame,
                    Nor blate nor scaur.

Whyles, ranging like a roaran lion,
For prey, a' holes an' corners tryin;
Whyles, on the strong-wing'd tempest flyin,
                    Tirlan the *kirks*;
Whyles, in the human bosom pryin,
                    Unseen thou lurks.

I've heard my rev'rend *Graunie* say,
In lanely glens ye like to stray;
Or where auld, ruin'd castles, gray,
                    Nod to the moon,

Ye fright the nightly wand'rer's way,
   Wi' eldritch croon.

When twilight did my *Graunie* summon,
To say her prayers, douse, honest woman!
Aft 'yont the dyke she's heard you bumman,
   Wi' eerie drone;
Or, rustling, thro' the boortries coman,
   Wi' heavy groan.

Ae dreary, windy, winter night,
The stars shot down wi' sklentan light,
Wi' you, *myself*, I gat a fright,
   Ayont the lough;
Ye, like a *rass-buss*, stood in sight,
   Wi' waving sugh.

The cudgel in my nieve did shake,
Each bristl'd hair stood like a stake,
When wi' an eldritch, stoor *quaick, quaick*,
   Amang the springs,
Awa ye squatter'd like a *drake*,
   On whistling wings.

Let *Warlocks* grim, an' wither'd *Hags*,
Tell how wi' you on ragweed nags,
They skim the muirs an' dizzy crags,
   Wi' wicked speed;
And in kirk-yards renew their leagues,
   Owre howcket dead.

Thence, countra wives, wi' toil an' pain,
May plunge an' plunge the *kirn* in vain;
For Oh! the yellow treasure's taen
   By witching skill;
An' dawtet, twal-pint *Hawkie's* gane
   As yell's the bill.

Thence, mystic knots mak great abuse,
On *Young-Guidmen*, fond, keen an' croose;

When the best *wark-lume* i' the house,
                          By cantraip wit,
Is instant made no worth a louse,
                          Just at the bit.

When thowes dissolve the snawy hoord,
An' float the jinglan icy boord,
Then *water-kelpies* haunt the foord,
                          By your direction,
An' nighted trav'llers are allur'd
                          To their destruction.

An' aft your moss-traversing *spunkies*
Decoy the wight that late an' drunk is:
The bleezan, curst, mischievous monkies
                          Delude his eyes,
Till in some miry slough he sunk is,
                          Ne'er mair to rise.

When Mason's mystic *word* an' *grip*,
In storms an' tempests raise you up,
Some cock or cat, your rage maun stop,
                          Or, strange to tell!
The *youngest brother* ye wad whip
                          Aff straught to Hell.

Lang syne in Eden's bonie yard,
When youthfu' lovers first were pair'd,
An' all the Soul of Love they shar'd,
                          The raptur'd hour,
Sweet on the fragrant, flow'ry swaird,
                          In shady bow'r.

Then you, ye auld, snick-drawing dog!
Ye cam to Paradise incog,
An' play'd on man a cursed brogue,
                          (Black be your fa'!)
An' gied the infant warld a shog,
                          'Maist ruin'd a'.

D'ye mind that day, when in a bizz,
Wi' reeket duds, an' reestet gizz,
Ye did present your smoutie phiz,
          'Mang better folk,
An' sklented on the *man of Uzz*,
          Your spitefu' joke?

An how ye gat him i' your thrall,
An' brak him out o' house an' hal',
While scabs an' botches did him gall,
          Wi' bitter claw,
An' lows'd his ill-tongu'd, wicked *scrawl*
          Was warst ava?

But a' your doings to rehearse,
Your wily snares an' fechtin fierce,
Sin' that day *Michael did you pierce,
          Down to this time,
Wad ding a *Lallan* tongue, or *Erse*,
          In Prose or Rhyme.

An' now, auld *Cloots*, I ken ye're thinkan,
A certain *Bardie's* rantin, drinkin,
Some luckless hour will send him linkan,
          To your black pit;
But faith! he'll turn a corner jinkan,
          An' cheat you yet.

But fare-you-weel, auld *Nickie-ben*!
O wad ye tak a thought an' men'!
Ye aiblens might – I dinna ken –
          Still hae a *stake* –
I'm wae to think upo' yon den,
          Ev'n for your sake!

*Vide Milton, [*Paradise Lost*] Book 6th. [RB]

To a Haggis

Fair fa' your honest, sonsie face,
Great Chieftan o' the Puddin-race!
Aboon them a' ye tak your place,
        Painch, tripe, or thairm:
Weel are ye wordy of a *grace*
        As lang's my arm.

The groaning trencher there ye fill,
Your hurdies like a distant hill,
Your *pin* wad help to mend a mill
        In time o' need,
While thro' your pores the dews distil
        Like amber bead.

His knife see Rustic-labour dight,
An' cut you up wi' ready slight,
Trenching your gushing entrails bright
        Like onie ditch;
And then, O what a glorious sight,
        Warm-reekin, rich!

Then, horn for horn they stretch an' strive,
Deil tak the hindmost, on they drive,
Till a' their weel-swall'd kytes belyve
        Are bent like drums;
Then auld Guidman, maist like to rive,
        Bethankit hums.

Is there that owre his French *ragout*,
Or *olio* that wad staw a sow,
Or *fricassee* wad mak her spew
        Wi' perfect sconner,
Looks down wi' sneering, scornfu' view
        On sic a dinner?

Poor devil! see him owre his trash,
As feckless as a wither'd rash,
His spindle-shank a guid whip-lash,
          His nieve a nit;
Thro' bluidy flood or field to dash,
          O how unfit!

But mark the Rustic, *haggis-fed*,
The trembling earth resounds his tread,
Clap in his walie nieve a blade,
          He'll mak it whissle;
An' legs, an' arms, an' heads will sned,
          Like taps o' thrissle.

Ye Pow'rs wha mak mankind your care,
An' dish them out their bill o' fare,
Auld Scotland wants nae skinking ware
          That jaups in luggies;
But, if ye wish her gratefu' pray'r,
          Gie her a *Haggis*!

My Peggy's Face

My Peggy's face, my Peggy's form,
The frost of hermit age might warm;
My Peggy's worth, my Peggy's mind,
Might charm the first of humankind.
I love my Peggy's angel air,
Her face so truly heavn'ly fair,
Her native grace so void of art,
But I adore my Peggy's heart.

The lily's hue, the rose's die,
The kindling lustre of an eye;
Who but owns their magic sway,
Who but knows they will decay!
The tender thrill, the pitying tear,
The gen'rous purpose nobly dear,
The gentle look that Rage disarms,
These are all Immortal charms.

O'er the Water to Charlie

(TUNE: SHAWNBOY)

Come boat me o'er, come row me o'er,
Come boat me o'er to Charlie;
I'll gie John Ross another bawbee,
To boat me o'er to Charlie.

> We'll o'er the water, we'll o'er the sea,
> We'll o'er the water to Charlie;
> Come weal, come woe, we'll gather and go,
> And live or die wi' Charlie.

I lo'e weel my Charlie's name,
Tho' some there be abhor him:
But O, to see auld Nick gaun hame,
And Charlie's faes before him!
> We'll o'er &c.

I swear and vow by moon and stars,
And sun that shines so early!
If I had twenty thousand lives,
I'd die as aft for Charlie.
> We'll o'er &c.

Auld Lang Syne

(TUNE: FOR OLD LONG SINE MY JO)

Should auld acquaintance be forgot
    And never brought to mind?
Should auld acquaintance be forgot,
    And auld lang syne!

    For auld lang syne my jo,
        For auld lang syne,
    We'll tak a *cup o' kindness yet,
        For auld lang syne.

And surely ye'll be your pint stowp!
    And surely I'll be mine!
And we'll tak a cup o' kindness yet,
    For auld lang syne.
           For auld &c.

We twa hae run about the braes,
    And pou'd the gowans fine;
But we've wander'd mony a weary fitt,
    Sin auld lang syne.
           For auld &c.

We twa hae paidl'd in the burn,
    Frae morning sun till dine;
But seas between us braid hae roar'd,
    Sin auld lang syne.
           For auld &c.

And there's a hand, my trusty fiere!
    And gie's a hand o' thine!
And we'll tak a right gude-willie-waught,
    For auld lang syne.
           For auld &c.

* Some sing, Kiss in place of Cup. [RB]

Elegy on the Year 1788

For Lords or kings I dinna mourn,
E'en let them die – for that they're born!
But oh! prodigious to reflect,
A *Towmont*, Sirs, is gane to wreck!
O *Eighty-eight*, in thy sma' space
What dire events ha'e taken place!
Of what enjoyments thou hast reft us!
In what a pickle thou has left us!

　The Spanish empire's tint a head,
An' my auld teethless Bawtie's dead;
The toolzie's teugh 'tween Pitt an' Fox,
An' our guidwife's wee birdy cocks;
The tane is game, a bluidy devil,
But to the *hen-birds* unco civil;
The tither's dour, has nae sic breedin',
But better stuff ne'er claw'd a midden!

　Ye ministers, come mount the pulpit,
An' cry till ye be haerse an' rupit;
For *Eighty-eight* he wish'd you weel,
An' gied you a' baith gear an' meal;
E'en mony a plack, an' mony a peck,
Ye ken ycoursels, for little feck!

　Ye bonny lasses, dight your een,
For some o' you ha'e tint a frien';
In *Eighty-eight*, ye ken, was ta'en
What ye'll ne'er ha'e to gi'e again.

　Observe the very nowt an' sheep,
How dowff an' dowie now they creep;
Nay, even the yirth itsel' does cry,
For Embro' wells are grutten dry.

24

O *Eighty-nine*, thou's but a bairn,
An' no owre auld, I hope, to learn!
Thou beardless boy, I pray tak' care,
Thou now has got thy Daddy's chair,

Nae hand-cuff'd, mizl'd, haff-shackl'd *Regent*,
But, like himsel', a full free agent.
Be sure ye follow out the plan
Nae war than he did, honest man!
As muckle better as you can.

January 1, 1789

Afton Water

Flow gently, sweet Afton, among thy green braes,
Flow gently, I'll sing thee a song in thy praise;
My Mary's asleep by thy murmuring stream,
Flow gently, sweet Afton, disturb not her dream.

Thou stock dove whose echo resounds thro' the glen,
Ye wild whistling blackbirds in yon thorny den,
Thou green crested lapwing thy screaming forbear,
I charge you disturb not my slumbering Fair.

How lofty, sweet Afton, thy neighbouring hills,
Far mark'd with the courses of clear, winding rills;
There daily I wander as noon rises high,
My flocks and my Mary's sweet cot in my eye.

How pleasant thy banks and green vallies below,
Where wild in the woodlands the primroses blow;
There oft as mild ev'ning weeps over the lea,
The sweet scented birk shades my Mary and me.

Thy chrystal stream, Afton, how lovely it glides,
And winds by the cot where my Mary resides;
How wanton thy waters her snowy feet lave,
As gath'ring sweet flow'rets she stems thy clear wave.

Flow gently, sweet Afton, among thy green braes,
Flow gently, sweet river, the theme of my lays;
My Mary's asleep by thy murmuring stream,
Flow gently, sweet Afton, disturb not her dream.

Tam O' Shanter. A Tale

Of Brownyis and of Bogillis full is this buke.
                                    Gawin Douglas

When chapman billies leave the street,
And drouthy neebors, neebors meet,
As market-days are wearing late,
An' folk begin to tak the gate;
While we sit bousing at the nappy,
An' getting fou and unco happy,
We think na on the lang Scots miles,
The mosses, waters, slaps and styles,
That lie between us and our hame,
Whare sits our sulky sullen dame,
Gathering her brows like gathering storm,
Nursing her wrath to keep it warm.

This truth fand honest *Tam o' Shanter*,
As he frae Ayr ae night did canter,
(Auld Ayr wham ne'er a town surpasses,
For honest men and bonny lasses.)

O *Tam*! hadst thou but been sae wise,
As ta'en thy ain wife *Kate's* advice!
She tauld thee weel thou was a skellum,
A blethering, blustering, drunken blellum;
That frae November till October,
Ae market day thou was nae sober;
That ilka melder, wi' the miller,
Thou sat as lang as thou had siller;
That ev'ry naig was ca'd a shoe on,
The smith and thee gat roaring fou on;
That at the Lord's house, ev'n on Sunday,
Thou drank wi' Kirkton Jean till Monday.
She prophesy'd that late or soon,

Thou would be found deep drown'd in Doon;
Or catch'd wi' warlocks in the mirk,
By *Alloway's* auld haunted kirk.

Ah, gentle dames! it gars me greet,
To think how mony counsels sweet,
How mony lengthen'd, sage advices,
The husband frae the wife despises!

But to our tale: Ae market night,
Tam had got planted unco right;
Fast by an ingle, bleezing finely,
Wi' reaming swats, that drank divinely;
And at his elbow, Souter *Johnny*,
His ancient, trusty, drouthy crony;
Tam lo'ed him like a vera brither;
They had been fou for weeks thegither.
The night drave on wi' sangs and clatter;
And ay the ale was growing better:
The landlady and *Tam* grew gracious,
Wi' favours, secret, sweet, and precious:
The Souter tauld his queerest stories;
The landlord's laugh was ready chorus:
The storm without might rair and rustle,
Tam did na mind the storm a whistle.

Care, mad to see a man sae happy,
E'en drown'd himself amang the nappy,
As bees flee hame wi' lades o' treasure,
The minutes wing'd their way wi' pleasure:
Kings may be blest, but *Tam* was glorious,
O'er a' the ills o' life victorious!

But pleasures are like poppies spread,
You seize the flow'r, its bloom is shed:
Or like the snow falls in the river,
A moment white – then melts forever;
Or like the borealis race,

That flit ere you can point their place;
Or like the rainbow's lovely form
Evanishing amid the storm. –
Nae man can tether time nor tide;
The hour approaches Tam maun ride;
That hour, o' night's black arch the key-stane,
That dreary hour he mounts his beast in;
And sic a night he taks the road in,
As ne'er poor sinner was abroad in.

The wind blew as 'twad blawn its last;
The rattling show'rs rose on the blast;
The speedy gleams the darkness swallow'd;
Loud, deep, and lang, the thunder bellow'd:
That night, a child might understand,
The Deil had business on his hand.

Weel mounted on his gray mare, *Meg*,
A better never lifted leg,
Tam skelpit on thro' dub and mire,
Despising wind, and rain, and fire;
Whiles holding fast his gude blue bonnet;
Whiles crooning o'er some auld Scots sonnet;
Whiles glow'ring round wi' prudent cares,
Lest bogles catch him unawares:
Kirk-Alloway was drawing nigh,
Whare ghaists and houlets nightly cry. –

By this time he was cross the ford,
Where in the snaw, the chapman smoor'd;
And past the birks and meikle stane,
Whare drunken *Charlie* brak's neck-bane;
And thro' the whins, and by the cairn,
Whare hunters fand the murder'd bairn;
And near the thorn, aboon the well,
Whare *Mungo's* mither hang'd hersel. –
Before him *Doon* pours all his floods:
The doubling storm roars thro' the woods:

The lightnings flash from pole to pole;
Near and more near the thunders roll:
When, glimmering thro' the groaning trees,
Kirk Alloway seem'd in a bleeze;
Thro' ilka bore the beams were glancing;
And loud resounded mirth and dancing. –

  Inspiring bold *John Barleycorn*!
What dangers thou canst make us scorn!
Wi' tipenny, we fear nae evil;
Wi' usquebae we'll face the devil! –
The swats sae ream'd in *Tammie's* noddle,
Fair play, he car'd na deils a boddle.
But *Maggie* stood right sair astonish'd,
Till, by the heel and hand admonish'd,
She ventur'd forward on the light;
And, vow! *Tam* saw an unco sight!
Warlocks and witches in a dance;
Nae cotillion brent new frae *France*,
But hornpipes, jigs, strathspeys, and reels,
Put life and mettle in their heels,
A winnock-bunker in the east,
There sat auld Nick, in shape o' beast;
A towzie tyke, black, grim, and large,
To gie them music was his charge:
He screw'd the pipes and gart them skirl,
Till roof and rafters a' did dirl. –
Coffins stood round, like open presses,
That shaw'd the dead in their last dresses;
And by some devilish cantraip slight
Each in its cauld hand held a light. –
By which heroic *Tam* was able
To note upon the haly table,
A murderer's banes in gibbet airns;
Twa span-lang, wee, unchristen'd bairns;
A thief, new-cutted frae a rape,
Wi' his last gasp his gab did gape;

Five tomahawks, wi' blude red-rusted;
Five scymitars, wi' murder crusted;
A garter, which a babe had strangled;
A knife, a father's throat had mangled,
Whom his ain son o' life bereft,
The grey hairs yet stack to the heft;
Wi' mair o' horrible an' awefu',
Which ev'n to name wad be unlawfu'.

As *Tammie* glowr'd, amaz'd, and curious,
The mirth and fun grew fast and furious;
The piper loud and louder blew;
The dancers quick and quicker flew;
They reel'd, they set, they cross'd, they cleekit,
Till ilka carlin swat and reekit,
And coost her duddies to the wark,
And linket at it in her sark!

Now *Tam*, O *Tam*! had thae been queans,
A' plump and strapping in their teens,
Their sarks, instead o' creeshie flannen,
Been snaw-white seventeen hunder linnen!
Thir breeks o' mine, my only pair,
That ance were plush, o' gude blue hair,
I wad hae gi'en them off my hurdies,
For ae blink o' the bonie burdies!

But wither'd beldams, auld and droll,
Rigwoodie hags wad spean a foal,
Lowping and flinging on a crummock,
I wonder didna turn thy stomach.

But *Tam* kend what was what fu' brawlie,
There was ae winsome wench and wawlie,
That night enlisted in the core,
(Lang after kend on *Carrick* shore;
For mony a beast to dead she shot,
And perish'd mony a bony boat,

And shook baith meikle corn and bear,
And kept the countryside in fear)
Her cutty sark, o' Paisley harn,
That while a lassie she had worn,
In longitude tho' sorely scanty,
It was her best, and she was vauntie. –
Ah! little kend thy reverend grannie,
That sark she coft for her wee Nannie,
Wi' twa pund Scots ('twas a' her riches)
Wad ever grac'd a dance o' witches!

But here my Muse her wing maun cour;
Sic flights are far beyond her pow'r;
To sing how Nannie lap and flang,
(A souple jade she was, and strang),
And how *Tam* stood, like ane bewitch'd,
And thought his very een enrich'd;
Ev'n Satan glowr'd, and fidg'd fu' fain,
And hotch'd and blew wi' might and main:
Till first ae caper, syne anither,
Tam tint his reason a' thegither,
And roars out, 'Weel done, Cutty-sark!'
And in an instant all was dark:
And scarcely had he Maggie rallied,
When out the hellish legion sallied.

As bees bizz out wi' angry fyke,
When plundering herds assail their byke,
As open pussie's mortal foes,
When pop! she starts before their nose;
As eager runs the market-crowd,
When 'Catch the thief!' resounds aloud;
So Maggie runs, the witches follow,
Wi' mony an eldritch skreech and hollow.

Ah, *Tam*! Ah, *Tam*! thou'll get thy fairin!
In hell they'll roast thee like a herrin!
In vain thy *Kate* awaits thy comin!

Kate soon will be a woefu' woman!
Now, do thy speedy utmost, Meg,
And win the key-stane* of the brig;
There at them thou thy tail may toss,
A running stream they dare na cross.
But ere the key-stane she could make,
The fient a tale she had to shake!
For Nannie, far before the rest,
Hard upon noble Maggie prest,
And flew at Tam wi' furious ettle;
But little wist she Maggie's mettle –
Ae spring brought off her master hale,
But left behind her ain gray tail:
The carlin claught her by the rump,
And left poor Maggie scarce a stump.

Now, wha this tale o' truth shall read,
Ilk man and mother's son, take heed:
Whene'er to drink you are inclin'd,
Or cutty sarks run in your mind,
Think, ye may buy the joys o'er dear,
Remember Tam o' Shanter's mare.

* It is a well known fact that witches, or any evil spirits, have no power to follow a poor wight any farther than the middle of the next running stream. – It may be proper likewise to mention to the benighted traveller, that when he falls in with *bogles*, whatever danger there may be in his going forward, there is much more hazard in turning back. [RB]

The Banks O' Doon

(TUNE: CALEDONIAN HUNT'S DELIGHT)

Ye banks and braes o' bonie Doon,
  How can ye bloom sae fresh and fair;
How can ye chant, ye little birds,
  And I sae weary fu' o' care!
Thou'll break my heart, thou warbling bird,
  That wantons thro' the flowering thorn:
Thou minds me o' departed joys,
  Departed never to return.

Oft hae I rov'd by bonie Doon,
  To see the rose and woodbine twine
And ilka bird sang o' its luve,
  And fondly sae did I o' mine.
Wi' lightsome heart I pu'd a rose,
  Fu' sweet upon its thorny tree;
And my fause luver staw my rose,
  But ah! he left the thorn wi' me.

Ae Fond Kiss

(TUNE: RORY DALL'S PORT)

Ae fond kiss, and then we sever;
Ae farewell and then forever!
Deep in heart-wrung tears I'll pledge thee,
Warring sighs and groans I'll wage thee.

Who shall say that fortune grieves him
While the star of hope she leaves him?
Me, nae chearfu' twinkle lights me;
Dark despair around benights me.

I'll ne'er blame my partial fancy,
Naething could resist my Nancy:
But to see her, was to love her;
Love but her, and love for ever.

Had we never lov'd sae kindly,
Had we never lov'd sae blindly,
Never met – or never parted,
We had ne'er been broken-hearted.

Fare thee weel, thou first and fairest!
Fare thee weel, thou best and dearest!
Thine be ilka joy and treasure,
Peace, Enjoyment, Love and Pleasure!

Ae fond kiss, and then we sever;
Ae fareweel, Alas! for ever!
Deep in heart-wrung tears I'll pledge thee,
Warring sighs and groans I'll wage thee.

Logan Water

O Logan, sweetly didst thou glide,
The day I was my Willie's bride;
And years sinsyne hae o'er us run,
Like Logan to the simmer sun.
But now thy flow'ry banks appear
Like drumlie winter, dark and drear,
While my dear lad maun face his faes,
Far, far frae me and Logan braes.

Again the merry month o' May
Has made our hills and vallies gay;
The birds rejoice in leafy bow'rs,
The bees hum round the breathing flow'rs:
Blythe morning lifts his rosy eye,
And ev'ning's tears are tears o' joy:
My soul, delightless, a' surveys,
While Willie's far frae Logan braes.

Within yon milk-white hawthorn bush,
Amang her nestlings sits the thrush;
Her faithfu' mate will share her toil,
Or wi' his song her cares beguile: —
But I, wi' my sweet nurslings here,
Nae mate to help, nae mate to cheer,
Pass widow'd nights, and joyless days,
While Willie's far frae Logan braes.

O wae upon you, men o' state,
That brethren rouse in deadly hate!
As ye make mony a fond heart mourn,
Sae may it on your heads return!
Ye mind na, mid your cruel joys,
The widow's tears, the orphan's cries!
But soon may peace bring happy days,
And Willie hame to Logan braes!

O, Whistle an' I'll Come to Ye, My Lad

O, whistle an' I'll come to ye, my lad!
O, whistle an' I'll come to ye, my lad!
Tho' father an' mother an' a' should gae mad,
O, whistle an' I'll come to ye, my lad!

But warily tent when ye come to court me,
And come nae unless the back-yett be a-jee;
Syne up the back-style, and let naebody see,
And come as ye were na comin to me.
And come as ye were na comin to me.

At kirk, or at market, whene'er ye meet me,
Gang by me as tho' that ye car'd na a flie;
But steal me a blink o' your bonie black e'e,
Yet look as ye were na looking to me.
Yet look as ye were na looking to me.

Ay vow and protest that ye care na for me,
And whiles ye may lightly my beauty awee;
But court na anither, tho' jokin ye be,
For fear that she wile your fancy frae me.
For fear that she wile your fancy frae me.

A Red, Red Rose

(TUNE: MAJOR GRAHAM)

My luve is like a red, red rose,
   That's newly sprung in June:
My luve is like the melodie,
   That's sweetly play'd in tune.
As fair art thou, my bonie lass,
   So deep in luve am I,
And I will luve thee still, my dear,
   Till a' the seas gang dry.

                  } [twice]

Till a' the seas gang dry, my dear,
   And the rocks melt wi' the sun!
And I will luve thee still, my dear,
   While the sands o' life shall run.
And fare-thee-weel, my only luve,
   And fare-thee-weel a while!
And I will come again, my luve,
   Tho' it were ten-thousand mile.

                  } [twice]

Ode to Spring

(TUNE: THE TITHER MORN)

When maukin bucks, at early f—s,
   In dewy glens are seen, Sir;
And birds, on boughs, take off their m—s,
   Amang the leaves sae green, Sir;
Latona's sun looks liquorish on
   Dame Nature's grand impètus,
Till his p—go rise, then westward flies
   To r—ger Madame Thetis.

Yon wandering rill that marks the hill,
   And glances o'er the brae, Sir,
Slides by a bower where many a flower
   Sheds fragrance on the day, Sir;
Thère Damon lay with Sylvia gay,
   To love they thought no crime, Sir;
The wild-birds sang, the echoes rang,
   While Damon's a—se beat time, Sir.

First, wi' the thrush, his thrust and push
   Had compass large and long, Sir;
The blackbird next, his tuneful text,
   Was bolder, clear and strong, Sir:
The linnet's lay came then in play,
   And the lark that soar'd aboon, Sir;
Till Damon, fierce, mistim'd his a—,
   And f—'d quite out o' tune, Sir.

Wantonness

Wantonness for ever mair,
Wantonness has been my ruin;
Yet for a' my dool and care,
It's wantonness for ever!

I hae lov'd the Black, the Brown,
I hae lov'd the Fair, the Gowden:
A' the colours in the town
I hae won their wanton favour.

Man Was Made to Mourn. A Dirge

(TUNE: PEGGY BAWN)

When chill November's surly blast
    Made fields and forests bare,
One ev'ning, as I wander'd forth,
    Along the banks of Aire,
I spy'd a man, whose aged step
    Seem'd weary, worn with care;
His face was furrow'd o'er with years,
    And hoary was his hair.

Young stranger, whither wand'rest thou?
    Began the rev'rend Sage;
Does thirst of wealth thy step constrain,
    Or youthful pleasure's rage?
Or haply, prest with cares and woes,
    Too soon thou hast began,
To wander forth, with me, to mourn
    The miseries of Man.

The sun that overhangs yon moors,
    Out-spreading far and wide,
Where hundreds labour to support
    A haughty lordling's pride;
I've seen yon weary winter-sun
    Twice forty times return;
And ev'ry time has added proofs,
    That Man was made to mourn.

O Man! while in thy early years,
    How prodigal of time!
Mispending all thy precious hours,
    Thy glorious, youthful prime!
Alternate follies take the sway;
    Licentious passions burn;

Which tenfold force gives Nature's law,
That Man was made to mourn.

Look not alone on youthful prime,
Or manhood's active might;
Man then is useful to his kind,
Supported is his right:
But see him on the edge of life,
With cares and sorrows worn,
Then age and want, Oh! ill-match'd pair!
Show Man was made to mourn.

A few seem favourites of Fate,
In pleasure's lap carest;
Yet think not all the Rich and Great,
Are likewise truly blest.
But Oh! what crouds in ev'ry land,
All wretched and forlorn,
Thro' weary life this lesson learn,
That Man was made to mourn!

Many and sharp the num'rous ills
Inwoven with our frame!
More pointed still we make ourselves,
Regret, remorse and shame!
And Man, whose heav'n-erected face,
The smiles of love adorn,
Man's inhumanity to Man
Makes countless thousands mourn!

See yonder poor, o'erlabour'd wight,
So abject, mean and vile,
Who begs a brother of the earth
To give him leave to toil;
And see his lordly *fellow-worm*,
The poor petition spurn,
Unmindful, tho' a weeping wife,
And helpless offspring mourn.

If I'm design'd yon lordling's slave,
   By Nature's law design'd,
Why was an independent wish
   E'er planted in my mind?
If not, why am I subject to
   His cruelty, or scorn?
Or why has Man the will and pow'r
   To make his fellow mourn?

Yet let not this too much, my son,
   Disturb thy youthful breast:
This partial view of human-kind
   Is surely not the *last*!
The poor, oppressed, honest man
   Had never, sure, been born,
Had there not been some recompense
   To comfort those that mourn!

O Death! the poor man's dearest friend,
   The kindest and the best!
Welcome the hour, my aged limbs
   Are laid with thee at rest!
The great, the wealthy fear thy blow,
   From pomp and pleasure torn;
But Oh! a blest relief for those
   That weary-laden mourn!

Holy Willie's Prayer

'And send the Godly in a pet to pray –' Pope

O Thou, wha in the heavens dost dwell,
Wha, as it pleases best thysel',
Sends ane to heaven and ten to hell,
      A' for thy glory,
And no for ony guid or ill
        They've done afore thee!

I bless and praise thy matchless might,
Whan thousands thou hast left in night,
That I am here afore thy sight,
      For gifts an' grace,
A burnin' an' a shinin' light,
        To a' this place.

What was I, or my generation,
That I should get such exaltation,
I wha deserve sic just damnation,
      For broken laws,
Five thousand years ere my creation,
        Thro' Adam's cause.

When frae my mither's womb I fell,
Thou might ha'e plunged me in hell,
To gnash my gums, to weep and wail,
      In burnin' lake,
Whar damned devils roar and yell,
        Chain'd to a stake.

Yet I am here a chosen sample,
To show thy grace is great an' ample;
I'm here a pillar in thy temple,
      Strong as a rock,
A guide, a buckler, an' example
        To a' thy flock.

44

But yet, O Lord! confess I must,
At times I'm fash'd wi' fleshly lust
An' sometimes too, wi' warldly trust,
        Vile Self gets in;
But thou remembers we are dust,
        Defil'd in sin.

O Lord! yestreen, thou kens, wi' Meg –
Thy pardon I sincerely beg –
O may't ne'er be a living plague
        To my dishonor!
An' I'll ne'er lift a lawless leg
        Again upon her.

Besides, I farther maun avow –
Wi' Leezie's lass, three times, I trow –
But, Lord, that Friday I was fou,
        When I cam near her,
Or else, thou kens, thy servant true
        Wad never steer her.

Maybe thou lets this fleshly thorn
Buffet thy servant e'en and morn,
Lest he owre proud and high should turn
        That he's sae gifted:
If sae, thy han' maun e'en be borne
        Until thou lift it.

Lord, bless thy Chosen in this place,
For here thou has a chosen race!
But God confound their stubborn face
        An' blast their name,
Wha bring thy elders to disgrace
        An' open shame!

Lord mind Gaun Hamilton's deserts,
He drinks, an' swears, an' plays at carts,
Yet has sae mony takin' arts,
        Wi' great an' sma'

Frae God's ain priest the people's hearts
          He steals awa'.

An' whan we chasten'd him therefore,
Thou kens how he bred sic a splore,
As set the warld in a roar
          O laughin' at us;
Curse thou his basket and his store,
          Kail an' potatoes.

Lord hear my earnest cry an' pray'r
Against that presbyt'ry o' Ayr;
Thy strong right hand, Lord make it bare,
          Upo' their heads,
Lord weigh it down, and dinna spare,
          For their misdeeds.

O Lord my God, that glib-tongu'd Aiken,
My very heart an' soul are quakin',
To think how we stood, sweatin', shakin',
          An' pissed wi' dread,
While Auld wi' hingin lip gaed sneakin',
          And hid his head.

Lord in the day of vengeance try him,
Lord visit them wha did employ him,
And pass not in thy mercy by 'em,
          Nor hear their prayer;
But for thy people's sake destroy 'em,
          And dinna spare.

But Lord remember me and mine
Wi' mercies temp'ral and divine,
That I for gear and grace may shine,
          Excell'd by nane,
An' a' the glory shall be thine,
          Amen, Amen.

The Twa Dogs. A Tale

'Twas in that place o' Scotland's isle,
That bears the name o' auld king Coil,
Upon a bonie day in June,
When wearing thro' the afternoon,
Twa Dogs, that were na thrang at hame,
Forgather'd ance upon a time.

The first I'll name, they ca'd him Caesar,
Was keepet for His Honor's pleasure;
His hair, his size, his mouth, his lugs,
Shew'd he was nane o' Scotland's dogs,
But whalpet some place far abroad,
Where sailors gang to fish for cod.

His locked, letter'd, braw brass-collar
Shew'd him the *gentleman* an' *scholar*;
But tho' he was o' high degree,
The fient a pride na pride had he,
But wad hae spent an hour caressan,
Ev'n wi' a Tinkler-gipsey's *messan*:
At kirk or market, mill or smiddie,
Nae tawted *tyke*, tho' e'er sae duddie,
But he wad stan't, as glad to see him,
An' stroan't on stanes an' hillocks wi' him.

The tither was a *ploughman's collie*,
A rhyming, ranting, raving billie,
Wha for his friend an' comrade had him,
And in his freaks had *Luath* ca'd him,
After some dog in *Highland sang,
Was made lang syne, lord knows how lang.

* Cuchullin's dog in Ossian's Fingal. [RB]

He was a gash an' faithfu' *tyke*,
As ever lap a sheugh or dyke.
His honest, sonsie, baws'nt face,
Ay gat him friends in ilka place;
His breast was white, his towsie back,
Weel clad wi' coat o' glossy black;
His gawsie tail, wi' upward curl,
Hung owre his hurdies wi' a swirl.

Nae doubt but they were fain o' ither,
An' unco pack an' thick thegither;
Wi' social nose whyles snuff'd an' snowket;
Whiles mice and modewurks they howket;
Whyles scour'd awa in lang excursion,
An' worry'd ither in diversion;
Till tir'd at last wi' mony a farce,
They set them down upon their arse,
An' there began a lang digression
About the *lords o' the creation*.

CAESAR

I've aften wonder'd, honest Luath,
What sort o' life poor dogs like you have;
An' when the *gentry* life I saw,
What way *poor bodies* liv'd ava.

Our *Laird* gets in his racked rents,
His coals, his kane, an' a' his stents:
He rises when he likes himsel;
His flunkies answer at the bell;
He ca's his coach; he ca's his horse;
He draws a bonie, silken purse
As lang's my tail, whare thro' the steeks,
The yellow letter'd *Geordie* keeks.

Frae morn to een it's nought but toiling,
At baking, roasting, frying, boiling;

An' tho' the gentry first are steghan,
Yet e'en the *ha' folk* fill their peghan
Wi' sauce, ragouts, and suc like trashtrie,
That's little short o' downright wastrie.
Our Whipper-in, wee blastiet wonner,
Poor, worthless elf, it eats a dinner,
Better than ony *Tenant-man*
His Honor has in a' the lan':
And what poor *Cot-folk* pit their painch in,
I own it's past my comprehension.

LUATH.

Trowth, Caesar, whyles they're fash't enough;
A *Cotter* howkan in a sheugh,
Wi' dirty stanes biggan a dyke,
Bairan a quarry, an' sic like,
Himsel, a wife, he thus sustains,
A smytrie o' wee, duddie weans,
An' nought but his han'-duark, to keep
Them right an' tight in thack an' raep.

An' when they meet wi' sair disasters,
Like loss o' health or want o' masters,
Ye maist wad think, a wee touch langer,
An' they maun starve o' cauld and hunger:
But how it comes, I never kent yet,
They're maistly wonderfu' contented;
An' buirdly chiels, and clever hizzies,
Are bred in sic a way as this is.

CAESAR

But then, to see how ye're negleket,
How huff'd, an' cuff'd, an' disrespeket!
Lord man, our gentry care as little
For *delvers*, *ditchers*, an sic cattle;
They gang as saucy by poor folk,
As I wad by a stinkan brock.

I've notic'd, on our Laird's *court-day*,
An' mony a time my heart's been wae,
Poor *tenant bodies*, scant o' cash,
How they maun thole a *factor's* snash;
He'll stamp an' threaten, curse an' swear,
He'll *apprehend* them, *poind* their gear;
While they maun stan', wi' aspect humble,
An' hear it a', an' fear an' tremble!

I see how folk live that hae riches;
But surely poor-folk maun be wretches!

LUATH

They're no sae wretched's ane wad think;
Tho' constantly on poortith's brink,
They're sae accustom'd wi' the sight,
The view o't gies them little fright.

Then chance and fortune are sae guided,
They're ay in less or mair provided;
An' tho' fatigu'd wi' close employment,
A blink o' rest's a sweet enjoyment.

The dearest comfort o' their lives,
Their grushie weans an' faithfu' wives;
The *prattling things* are just their pride,
That sweetens a' their fire-side.

An' whyles twalpennie-worth o' *nappy*
Can mak the bodies unco happy;
They lay aside their private cares,
To mind the Kirk and State affairs;
They'll talk o' *patronage* an' *priests*,
Wi' kindling fury i' their breasts,
Or tell what new taxation's comin,
An' ferlie at the folk in Lon'on.

As bleak-fac'd Hallowmass returns,
They get the jovial, rantan *Kirns*,
When *rural life*, of ev'ry station,
Unite in common recreation;
Love blinks, Wit slaps, an' social Mirth
Forgets there's *care* upo' the earth.

That *merry day* the year begins,
They bar the door on frosty win's;
The nappy reeks wi' mantling ream,
An' sheds a heart-inspiring steam;
The luntan pipe, an' sneeshin mill,
Are handed round wi' right guid will;
The cantie auld folks, crackan crouse,
The young anes rantan thro' the house –
My heart has been sae fain to see them,
That I for joy hae barket wi' them.

Still it's owre true that ye hae said,
Sic game is now owre aften play'd;
There's monie a creditable *stock*
O' decent, honest, fawsont folk,
Are riven out baith root an' branch,
Some rascal's pridefu' greed to quench,
Wha thinks to knit himself the faster
In favor wi' some *gentle Master*,
Wha aiblens thrang a *parliamentin*,
For Britain's guid his saul indentin –

CAESAR

Haith lad, ye little ken about it;
For Britain's guid! guid faith! I doubt it.
Say rather, gaun as Premiers lead him,
An' saying *aye* or *no*'s they bid him:
At operas an' plays parading,
Mortgaging, gambling, masquerading:
Or maybe in a frolic daft,

To Hague or Calais takes a waft,
To make a *tour* an' tak a whirl,
To learn *bon ton* an' see the worl'.

There at Vienna or Versailles,
He rives his father's auld entails,
Or by Madrid he takes the rout,
To thrum *guittars* an' fecht wi' nowt;
Or down *Italian vista* startles,
Wh-re-hunting amang groves o' myrtles:
Then bowses drumlie *German-water*,
To mak himsel look fair and fatter,
An' purge the bitter ga's an' cankers,
O' curst *Venetian* bores and chancres.

For Britain's guid! for her destruction!
Wi' dissipation, feud an' faction!

LUATH

Hech man! dear sirs! is that the gate,
They waste sae mony a braw estate!
Are we sae foughten and harass'd
For gear to gang that gate at last!

O would they stay aback frae courts,
An' please themsels wi' countra sports,
It wad for ev'ry ane be better,
The *Laird*, the *Tenant*, an' the *Cotter*!
For thae frank, rantan, ramblan billies,
Fient haet o' them's ill-hearted fellows;
Except for breakin o' their timmer,
Or speakin lightly o' their *Limmer*,
Or shootin of a hare or moorcock,
The ne'er-a-bit they're ill to poor folk.

But will ye tell me, master Caesar,
Sure *great folk*'s life's a life o' pleasure?
Nae cauld nor hunger e'er can steer them,
The vera thought o't need na fear them.

CAESAR

Lord man, were ye but whyles where I am,
The *gentles* ye wad neer envy them!

It's true, they need na starve or sweat,
Thro' Winter's cauld, or Summer's heat;
They've nae sair-wark to craze their banes,
An' fill *auld-age* wi' grips an' granes;
But *human-bodies* are sic fools,
For a' their colledges an' schools,
That when nae *real* ills perplex them,
They *mak* enow themsels to vex them;
An' ay the less they hae to sturt them,
In like proportion, less will hurt them.

A country fellow at the pleugh,
His *acre's* till'd, he's right eneugh;
A country girl at her wheel,
Her *dizzen's* done, she's unco weel;
But Gentlemen, an' Ladies warst,
Wi' ev'n down *want o' wark* are curst.
They loiter, lounging, lank an' lazy;
Tho' deil-haet ails them, yet uneasy;
Their days, insipid, dull an' tasteless,
Their nights, unquiet, lang an' restless.

An ev'n their sports, their balls an' races,
Their galloping thro' public places,
There's sic parade, sic pomp an' art,
The joy can scarcely reach the heart.

The *Men* cast out in *party-matches*,
Then sowther a' in deep debauches.
Ae night, they're mad wi' drink an' wh-ring,
Niest day their life is past enduring.

The *Ladies* arm-in-arm in clusters,
As great an' gracious a' as sisters;

But hear their *absent thoughts* o' ither,
They're a run deils an' jads thegither.
Whyles, owre the wee bit cup an' platie,
They sip the *scandal-potion* pretty;
Or lee-lang nights, wi' crabbet leuks,
Pore owre the devil's *pictur'd beuks*;
Stake on a chance a farmer's stackyard,
An' cheat like ony *unhang'd blackguard.*

There's some exceptions, man an' woman;
But this is Gentry's life in common.

By this, the sun was out o' sight,
An' darker gloamin brought the night:
The *bum-clock* humm'd wi' lazy drone,
The kye stood rowtan i' the loan;
When up they gat an' shook their lugs,
Rejoic'd they were na *men* but *dogs*;
An' each took off his several way,
Resolv'd to meet some ither day.

Farewell to the Highlands

(TUNE: *FAILTE NA MIOSG* – THE MUSKET SALUTE)

My heart's in the Highlands, my heart is not here;
My heart's in the Highlands a chasing the deer;
A chasing the wild deer, and following the roe,
My heart's in the Highlands, wherever I go.
Farewell to the Highlands, farewell to the north,
The birth place of Valour, the country of Worth,
Wherever I wander, wherever I rove,
The hills of the Highlands for ever I love.
Farewell to the mountains high cover'd with snow;
Farewell to the straths and green vallies below:
Farewell to the forests and wild hanging woods;
Farewell to the torrents and loud pouring floods.
My heart's in the Highlands, my heart is not here,
My heart's in the Highlands, a chasing the deer:
Chasing the wild deer, and following the roe,
My heart's in the Highlands, wherever I go.

John Anderson My Jo

John Anderson my jo, John,
When we were first acquent;
Your locks were like the raven,
Your bony brow was brent;
But now your brow is beld, John,
Your locks are like the snaw;
But blessings on your frosty pow,
John Anderson my jo.

John Anderson my jo, John,
We clamb the hill the gither;
And mony a canty day, John,
We've had wi' ane anither:
Now we maun totter down, John,
And hand in hand we'll go:
And sleep the gither at the foot,
John Anderson my jo.

Scots Wha Hae

(TUNE: HEY, TUTTI TAITIE)

Scots, wha hae wi' Wallace bled,
Scots, wham Bruce has aften led,
Welcome to your gory bed
      Or to victorie!

Now's the day, and now's the hour:
See the front o' battle lour,
See approach proud Edward's power –
      Chains and slaverie!

Wha will be a traitor knave?
Wha can fill a coward's grave?
Wha sae base as be a slave? –
      Let him turn, and flee!

Wha for Scotland's king and law
Freedom's sword will strongly draw,
Freeman stand or freeman fa',
      Let him follow me!

By Oppression's woes and pains,
By your sons in servile chains,
We will drain our dearest veins
      But they shall be free!

Lay the proud usurpers low!
Tyrants fall in every foe!
Liberty's in every blow! –
      Let us do, or die!

Is There for Honest Poverty

(TUNE: FOR A' THAT)

Is there for honest poverty
   That hings his head, an' a' that?
The coward slave, we pass him by –
   We dare be poor for a' that!
      For a' that, an a' that,
         Our toils obscure, an' a' that,
      The rank is but the guinea's stamp,
         The man's the gowd for a' that.

What tho' on hamely fare we dine,
   Wear hodden grey, an' a' that?
Gie fools their silks, and knaves their wine –
   A man's a man for a' that!
      For a' that, an' a' that,
         Their tinsel show, an' a' that,
      The honest man, tho' e'er sae poor,
         Is king o' men for a' that.

Ye see yon birkie ca'd a lord,
   Wha struts, and stares, an' a' that;
Tho' hundreds worship at his word,
   He's but a coof for a' that.
      For a' that, an' a' that,
         His ribband, star, an' a' that,
      The man o' independent mind,
         He looks an' laughs at a' that.

A prince can mak a belted knight,
   A marquis, duke, an' a' that,
But an honest man's aboon his might –
   Gude faith, he mauna fa' that!
      For a' that, an' a' that,
         Their dignities, an a' that,

The pith o' sense an' pride o' worth
    Are higher rank than a' that.

Then let us pray that come it may –
    As come it will, for a' that –
That sense and worth, o'er a' the earth
    Shall bear the gree, an' a' that;
        For a' that, an' a' that,
          It's comin yet for a' that,
        That man to man the world o'er,
          Shall brothers be for a' that.